LET'S PRAY

Thankful Heart Prayer Prompts

by
Sophia Lilyquist

Let's Pray (Thankful Heart Prayer Prompts)

Copyright © 2021 by Sophia Lilyquist. All rights reserved.

No portion of this book may be reproduced, stored in a retrieval system, or transmitted in any form or by any means- electronic, mechanical, photocopy, recording, scanning, or other - except for brief quotations in critical reviews or articles, without the prior written permission.

ISBN: 978-1-7377421-1-1

Scripture quotations taken from

The Holy Bible, New International Version® NIV®
Copyright © 1973, 1978, 1984, 2011 by Biblica, Inc.®
Used by Permission of Biblica, Inc.® All rights reserved worldwide.

Holy Bible, New Living Translation
Copyright 1996, 2004, 2007, 2015 by Tyndale House Foundation.
Used by permission of Tyndale House Publishers, Inc., Carol Stream, Illinois, 60188. All rights reserved.

 Authors' note: Thank you for buying this book.
Profits from this book will help feed a hungry child in India.

Give thanks to the LORD, for he is good;
His love endures forever.
Psalm 107:1

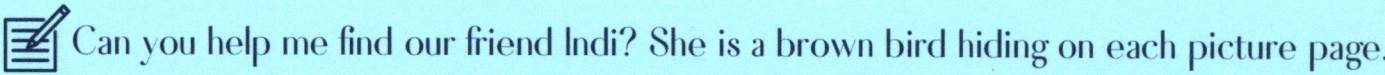 Can you help me find our friend Indi? She is a brown bird hiding on each picture page.

From the rising of the sun to its setting, the name of the Lord is to be praised!
Psalm 113:3

....

....

....

 What are you thankful for? Write your own prayer points or praise report.

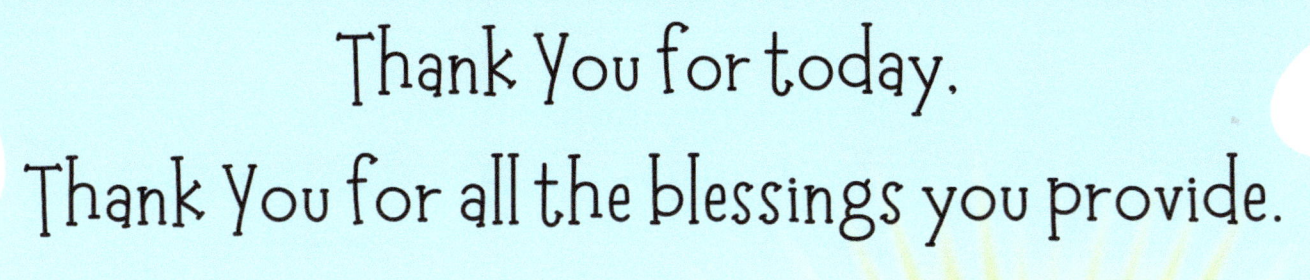

Thank You for today.
Thank You for all the blessings you provide.

Honor your father and mother.
Ephesians 6:2

 Ask mommy and/or daddy for their prayer needs.

May God be merciful and bless us.
May his face smile with favor on us.
Psalm 67:1

 Do you have any answered prayers you can write here?

Thank You for my brothers/sisters.
Help us to be loving and kind to each other every single day.

Praise the Lord, my soul, and forget not all his benefits -who forgives all your sins and heals all your diseases.
Psalm 103:2-3

•···•

•···•

•···•

 Do your grandparents have prayer needs?
Write them above so you can remember to pray for them.

The Lord is my rock, my fortress, and my deliverer; my God is my rock, in whom I take refuge.
Psalm 18:2

List your friends' and families' names here.
Don't forget to pray for those who do not know Jesus yet.

Thank You for my cousins and friends.
Thank You for keeping us safe.

So whether you eat or drink, or whatever you do,
do it all for the glory of God.
1 Corinthians 10:31

•⋯⋯⋯⋯⋯⋯⋯⋯⋯⋯⋯⋯⋯⋯⋯⋯⋯⋯⋯⋯⋯⋯⋯⋯⋯⋯⋯⋯⋯•

•⋯⋯⋯⋯⋯⋯⋯⋯⋯⋯⋯⋯⋯⋯⋯⋯⋯⋯⋯⋯⋯⋯⋯⋯⋯⋯⋯⋯⋯•

•⋯⋯⋯⋯⋯⋯⋯⋯⋯⋯⋯⋯⋯⋯⋯⋯⋯⋯⋯⋯⋯⋯⋯⋯⋯⋯⋯⋯⋯•

📝 What has God blessed you with?

Did you know this book helps feed hungry children?

Thank You, God, for the food that helps me to be healthy, and thank You for all the snacks I get to enjoy.

In peace I will lie down and sleep,
for you alone, O Lord, will keep me safe.
Psalm 4:8

 Thank you for praying for those who don't have a home.
You can ask your parents how you can help.

Thank You for my house.
Thank You for helping me get a good night's sleep.

God, please help those who don't have their own house or food.

For God so loved the world that he gave his one and only
Son, that whoever believes in him
shall not perish but have eternal life.
John 3:16

•⋯⋯⋯⋯⋯⋯⋯⋯⋯⋯⋯⋯⋯⋯⋯⋯⋯⋯⋯⋯⋯⋯⋯⋯⋯⋯⋯⋯⋯⋯⋯⋯⋯⋯•

•⋯⋯⋯⋯⋯⋯⋯⋯⋯⋯⋯⋯⋯⋯⋯⋯⋯⋯⋯⋯⋯⋯⋯⋯⋯⋯⋯⋯⋯⋯⋯⋯⋯⋯•

•⋯⋯⋯⋯⋯⋯⋯⋯⋯⋯⋯⋯⋯⋯⋯⋯⋯⋯⋯⋯⋯⋯⋯⋯⋯⋯⋯⋯⋯⋯⋯⋯⋯⋯•

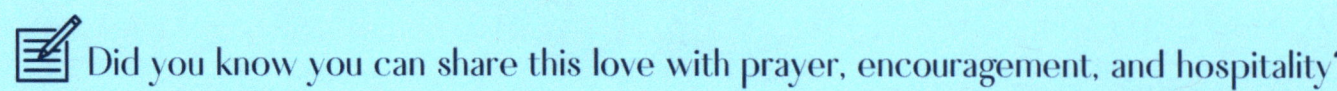 Did you know you can share this love with prayer, encouragement, and hospitality?

Thank You, God for saving us from our sins and showing us how to love.
In the name of Jesus, I pray
Amen!

Our **Father** in **Heaven**,
hallowed be your name.
Your **kingdom** come,
Your **will** be **done**, on **earth** as in **heaven**.
Give us today our **daily bread**.
Forgive us our sins, as we **forgive** those
who sin against **us**.
Lead us not into **temptation**,
but **deliver** us from evil.
For the **kingdom**, the **power**, and the **glory** are yours,
Now and **Forever**. Amen.
Matthew 6:9-13

About the Author

Sophia Lilyquist is a self-taught illustrator who is passionate about helping children understand the love of God.

Born and raised in Tamil Nadu, India, having a pastor and philanthropist for a dad meant Sophia had a front-row seat to learn values that include the contribution of time and talent. As a young lady, she continued to serve in various social roles. She now serves as the Executive Director of Love and Care Ministries International.

Let's Pray: Thankful Heart Prayer Prompts is her debut book.

You can learn more about her and how this book helps feed children by visiting the website.

lnci.org/sophia